Shark Lady

Shark Lady

True Adventures of Eugenie Clark

by Ann McGovern

illustrated by Ruth Chew

Scholastic Inc.
New York Toronto London Auckland Sydney

For May Garelick,
    who led me to the right door.

For Barbara and Fred Brenner,
    whose door opened to a new world.

For Marty Scheiner,
    who is the major person in that world.

Cover photos by David Doubilet.

ISBN 0-590-44771-8

12 11 10   7 8 9/9

Contents

A Very Special Saturday

"Wake up, Genie," Mama called. "We have to go downtown soon."

Eugenie Clark mumbled into her pillow. Who wants to go downtown on a Saturday? Saturdays were for climbing rocks and trees with Norma, her best friend. Saturdays were for digging up fat worms, bringing home bugs and snakes — making sure that Grandma didn't see them.

Those were the good Saturdays. But today was different. Her friend Norma had to go shopping with her mother.

Grandma wasn't feeling well and needed peace and quiet. There was no place for nine-year-old Eugenie to be except with Mama at work.

Mama worked in a big building in downtown New York City. She sold newspapers at the newsstand in the lobby.

In the rumbling subway train speeding downtown, Mama looked at her daughter's sad face and wished there was something she could do to make Eugenie happier.

Eugenie's father had died when she was a baby. So Mama had to work extra hard to earn enough money to take care of the family. Working extra hard meant working Saturday mornings, too.

The subway train pulled into their station and they got out. A sign at the top of the subway stairs said: TO THE AQUARIUM.

"A good idea," Mama said. "I'll leave you at the Aquarium and I'll pick you up at lunchtime. That will be more fun for you than sitting around the newsstand all morning."

Eugenie walked through the doors of the Aquarium and into the world of fish.

She walked among the tanks filled with strange fish. Then she came to a big, mysterious looking tank at the back. She stared at it for a long, long time. The green misty water seemed to go on and on. She leaned over the rail, her face close to the glass, and pretended that she was walking on the bottom of the sea.

Eugenie went to the Aquarium the next Saturday. And the next Saturday. And the Saturday after that. She went to the Aquarium on all the cold Saturdays, the rainy and snowy Saturdays of autumn and winter. Some-

times her best friend, Norma, came with her. But often she was alone with the fish.

Eugenie read about fish, too. She read about a scientist who put a diving helmet on his head and went deep under the waves. He walked on the bottom of the sea with the fish swimming around him.

"Someday I'll walk with the fish, too," she said.

In the summertime, Mama took her to the beach. Mama had taught Eugenie to swim before she was two years old.

When Mama came out of the water, her long jet-black hair streamed down her back. Eugenie thought Mama looked like pictures she had seen of beautiful pearl divers of the Orient. Mama was Japanese.

Mama was a good swimmer, and in the summertime Eugenie loved to watch her swim with long, graceful strokes.

Now, in the autumn and in the winter, Eugenie watched the very best swimmers — the fish in the Aquarium. She found all the fish fascinating — the smallest fish glowing like tiny jewels and the fish with fluttering fins that looked like fairy wings. But it was the biggest streamlined fish in the Aquarium that she came back to again and again.

She watched the big shark swimming, turning, swimming, turning, never resting its long, graceful body. She watched it and lost track of time.

"Mysterious shark," she thought. "Someday I'll swim with sharks, too."

Three Fish, Four Fish—More and More Fish

"Good morning, Genie. Great weather for fish," the guard at the Aquarium said one rainy Saturday.

Eugenie laughed. "Hi, Mr. Walker. Are my friends here yet?"

Mr. Walker nodded. "Oh yes," he said. "They always show up on rainy days." He watched the skinny dark-haired girl go through the door.

"Friends, ha!" he thought. "Those good-for-nothing bums that come here to get out of the rain." Mr. Walker shook his head. "Never saw anything like it. A bunch of bums paying attention to a little girl talking about fish!"

Inside the Aquarium, Eugenie moved from one fish tank to another. A small group of men in dirty, worn-out clothes followed her.

"Hey, teacher," one man said, "this fish has whiskers, just like mine."

"Like the whiskers on a cat, too," Eugenie said. "Maybe that's why it's called a catfish. See? Watch how it uses its whiskers to find food on the bottom of the tank."

The men always called her *teacher*, half in fun. One of her secret dreams was to be a teacher like wonderful Miss Reilly, her favorite teacher in all the world.

Miss Reilly took Eugenie's fourth-grade class on field trips to the woods to gather moss, ferns, and salamanders. Eugenie hoped that they could come to the Aquarium, too. Miss

Reilly had said she would like the class to see "Genie's fish."

"Genie's fish. Genie's fish." An idea began to grow.

And the next Saturday at lunchtime, the idea spilled out. Every Saturday, Eugenie and Mama ate lunch at a tiny Japanese restaurant owned by their good friend, Nobusan.

Today, Eugenie's mind was whirling with her new idea.

"Just think," she said. "Some people have beautiful fish in their own home and watch them all the time. Mama, Christmas is coming soon." Eugenie crossed her fingers and made a wish.

After lunch, Eugenie and Mama went to a pet shop to pick out the Christmas present. They chose a large aquarium with gravel and stones. They bought plants to make it look natural. They bought some snails to keep it clean.

Then came the best part — picking out the fish. They chose guppies and angelfish, green swordtails and black-speckled red-fish.

"Stop!" Eugenie's mother laughed. "I've spent more than I planned for Christmas." Just then Eugenie saw a red-banded clownfish. "Oh, Mama, could I have just one more," she begged, "for my birthday?"

"But your birthday isn't until May,"
Mama said. The clownfish swam to
the front of the tank. "It is pretty,"
Mama said. "All right, we'll buy it."

Before they left the shop that day
they lost track of how many years'
worth of Christmas and birthday
presents Eugenie had in advance.

Before long, the small apartment was crowded with fish of all kinds. Mama became fascinated with fish, too. Sometimes she would bring home little white boxes with fish swimming inside. When that happened, Eugenie knew that Mama had spent her lunch

hour and maybe her lunch money in the pet shop.

Eugenie joined the Queens County Aquarium Society and became its youngest member. She learned how to keep good records of her pets. She wrote down their scientific names, the dates she got each fish, and what happened to them.

When some of Eugenie's fish had babies, hundreds of tiny wriggling fish filled the aquarium. Once Eugenie thought of going into the fish business selling baby fish.

But Grandma said NO!

Trouble With Grandma

Eugenie's zoo grew. Besides hundreds of fish, there were salamanders, toads, and snakes.

When Eugenie went to college, she was more interested in fish than in any other animal. But in order to learn about fish, she had to study all kinds of creatures.

She learned how to cut up — *dissect* — dead animals, which is the best way to find out about their different parts.

Once a friendly pet-shop owner

gave Eugenie a monkey that had died. She took it home and put it in the refrigerator so it wouldn't spoil and smell bad. That evening, Grandma opened the refrigerator door and saw the dead monkey on the shelf. She screamed and ran out of the kitchen. "No more dead animals in this house!" she said.

"Why doesn't Genie study typing?" she complained to Mama. Mama worried, too.

"Genie dear," she said, "I know you want to study and work with fish — to be an *ichthyologist*. But what if you can't be an ichthyologist right away? If you learn typing you might be able to be the secretary of a famous ichthyologist."

But Eugenie knew what she wanted to be. And so she went right on studying hard and learning about fish and other animals.

Eugenie had learned how to skin a dead animal in the lab in college, but she felt she needed more practice. One day the neighborhood grocer killed a big rat in his store and Eugenie begged to have it.

The grocer wrapped it up and she took it home. Good. There was nobody in the house. Quickly Eugenie skinned it. Then she got out one of her grandmother's cooking pots.

She wanted the skeleton. She would have to boil the rat. Every five minutes Eugenie ran into the street to see if Grandma was coming. Then she ran into the house again and checked the pot. The rat was still boiling on the stove when Eugenie suddenly heard Grandma's footsteps outside.

What could Eugenie *do*?

It was too late to do anything. Grandma was standing in the kitchen doorway.

"Genie, darling," she said. "What are you cooking?"

Before Eugenie could stop her, she lifted the pot cover, peered inside, and saw the big rat's two sharp teeth.

Grandma was very angry. And Eugenie was not allowed to cook in the kitchen again for a long time.

Danger in the Deep

Eugenie graduated from Hunter College in New York City. She went to California to go on with her fish studies and to work as a part-time research assistant to Dr. Carl Hubbs, a famous ichthyologist.

In those days, people who wanted to explore the bottom of the sea had to wear heavy helmets with air lines that connected them to the boat above.

Now, for the first time, Eugenie

was going to walk on the sea bottom in a diving helmet!

Before Eugenie could go in the water, she had to have lessons. She had to learn how to turn the air valve on the helmet to control the amount of air she breathed.

She had to know about the signals that the divers used to send messages to the boat. One tug on the signal line meant: "I'm okay." Two tugs meant: "Give me more line." Three tugs meant: "Take up the loose line," and four tugs meant: "Danger. Pull me up." And most important, she had to stay calm in case of an emergency.

At last she was ready. She climbed down the boat's ladder until she was up to her neck in water. Then the heavy helmet was put on her head.

She slid down the rope until her feet touched sand. She was really on the bottom of the sea! Silvery fish swam by, so close! One fish swam right up to her helmet and looked in at her face.

Once the sand moved under her feet and a flounder darted away. Everything seemed magical — even a clump of rocks. Coming closer she could see that the rocks had holes like windows, with lovely fish darting in

and out. Colorful sponges grew over the rocks. "Like Hänsel and Gretel's gingerbread house in a water forest," she thought. "I wonder what witch of the sea lives here."

She remembered the first time she went to the Aquarium, when she had pretended to be walking on the bottom of the sea.

"Now I'm not pretending. I am really, really walking on the bottom of the sea."

She wandered along the sea bottom as if in a dream. She tried to catch some of the bold fish with her hands.

Suddenly she noticed that it was getting harder to breathe. She turned the air valve on her helmet, but it didn't help. Soon she was gasping for air. She opened the valve more and more until it no longer turned.

Her head felt groggy. Something was terribly wrong. She started toward the boat as fast as she could. But her steps were so slow. The helmet was so heavy. Now her breath was coming in short gasps. Her eyes burned. Her head felt numb.

At last she saw the bottom of the boat. Now she could see the line hanging under the boat. With her last bit of strength, she tugged hard. Four tugs meant *Danger. Pull me up*! But she could tug on the line only once before she felt herself falling. As she fell to her knees, she thought, "No! One tug means *okay*. I'm not okay . . . *not* okay."

Now water was beginning to seep into her helmet — cold water that brought her to her senses. As fast as she could, she got the heavy helmet off her head and let herself float up, up, up to the surface.

The men on the boat dived over the side. Strong hands reached out to her.

Safe on board, she was wrapped in warm blankets and given hot coffee.

"What happened?" Dr. Hubbs asked, when she was rested.

Eugenie told him about her breathing trouble. "I kept opening the valve more and more, but no more air came in," she said.

A sailor on the boat laughed. "I bet you screwed the valve the wrong way and cut off your own air," he said. "Just like a girl."

Dr. Hubbs checked the diving helmet. "Wait a minute, sailor," he said. "Who was responsible for checking the air line? There's a leak in it. That means she was losing most of the air before it could even get into her helmet."

The sailor's face turned red. "Sorry," he mumbled.

"What a terrible thing to happen on your first dive," Dr. Hubbs said to Eugenie. "There's only one thing to do."

And that one thing was to go down to the bottom of the sea again. So as soon as the helmet was fixed, down, down, she went. And this time — as in all the helmet dives to follow — nothing went wrong.

Adventures in the South Seas

After studying and working with Dr. Hubbs in California for almost a year, Eugenie went back to New York. She worked at the Museum of Natural History and studied at New York University.

Now, three years later, she was saying good-bye to Mama and her stepfather, Nobusan. Mama had married Nobusan, whom Eugenie had loved ever since she was a child.

Eugenie was flying far away to the South Sea Islands. The U.S. Navy and scientists in Washington wanted to learn more about the fish of these Pacific Islands. Which ones were safe to eat? Which ones were poisonous? Would Eugenie Clark be willing to fly 9,000 miles* to collect fish and study them? Would she! She could hardly wait.

The next few months were filled with adventure. She traveled from island to island collecting fish in the beautiful blue-green waters of the coral reefs. She wore a glass face mask so she could keep her eyes open and see clearly underwater. With her *snorkel* she could float on the top of the water for a long time and look down through her mask at the wonders of the Pacific reefs below.

She went diving with the native fishermen of the islands. They shared their lunches of raw fish with her and the cool white milk of coconuts.

* 14,400 kilometers

Eugenie made friends on every island.

On the tiny island of Mog Mog, Eugenie was taken to meet King Ueg. He was the first king she had ever known. What would he think of her in her bare feet, her hair in pigtails, and wearing only her bathing suit? But the King didn't mind. He wasn't wearing anything but a loincloth!

On another island she made friends with the Governor and his family. The whole family helped her collect fish on the reef. The collecting trips became picnics. At night they all pitched in to sort out the fish and take notes.

Eugenie learned many things about the poisonous fish of the South Seas. She learned that some fish might be poisonous on one island but not on another. She learned that some fish were dangerous to eat at certain times of the year but perfectly safe at other times.

Eugenie never knew what adventures she would face each day. One afternoon she was in the water collecting fish. She had been swimming a long time and she was tired. She was far out on the reef where the water was very deep.

Suddenly she sensed something behind her. She turned. A big shark was swimming toward her!

She stopped swimming. The shark was coming closer and closer. Eugenie knew she should be frightened. Her mind told her to be frightened. But she wasn't. All she could do was admire the shark. It was so streamlined, so graceful. The shark came so close to her that she could almost have reached out and touched it. Then it turned and swam off, down into the deep.

Suddenly Eugenie remembered the promise she had made to herself long ago. "Someday I'll swim with sharks," she had said when she was a little girl at the Aquarium in New York City.

Now that dream, too, had come true.

Fishing for Sharks

Eugenie was back in New York City. Snow was falling softly outside her window. She was thinking of warmer days in warm waters.

So much had happened since she had seen her first shark in the waters of the South Sea Islands.

Eugenie had gone on with her studies in ichthyology and had earned high honors. Now she was called *Dr. Eugenie Clark!* She had won scholarships to study fish in many parts of the world. And she had married a doctor. Best of all, they had Hera, a darling baby girl. Somehow Dr. Eugenie Clark had also found time to write a book about her adventures — *Lady With a Spear*.

In her book, she had written about a marine laboratory on the Red Sea where she studied and worked for a year.

Thousands of people read her book. Anne and William Vanderbilt of Florida read it, too.

There was no marine laboratory in the western part of Florida where the Vanderbilts lived. They called Eugenie and invited her to meet with them.

"It would be great if we had a marine lab here," Mr. Vanderbilt said to her, "something like the one you described in your book. What do you think? Would you consider starting one and being the director?"

Her own lab! It was a thrilling thought.

"Make it a place where people can learn more about the sea," Mr. Vanderbilt said. The Vanderbilts were very rich. They used some of their money for worthwhile projects, like the Marine Laboratory.

Eugenie's husband liked the idea of being a doctor in Florida. The warm Florida sunshine would be wonderful for little Hera and for the new baby who would soon be born. Even Mama and Nobusan were excited. "Maybe we'll move down and open a restaurant," Mama said. "There isn't one Japanese restaurant in the state of Florida."

Six months later, in early January, 1955, Dr. Eugenie Clark opened the doors of a small wooden building. A sign over the door said *Cape Haze*

Marine Laboratory. Nearby were beaches, bays, islands, and the Gulf of Mexico. And the sea was right outside the door!

Eugenie couldn't wait to see what treasures were in those waters. That very afternoon she and a local fisherman, Beryl Chadwick, netted many fish, including sea horses. Eugenie was eager to start the job of identifying all the local fishes. Beryl would be her assistant.

The very next day, Eugenie got a phone call from a Dr. John Heller. He needed shark livers for his important medical research. He had heard about the new lab. Could Eugenie possibly get him a shark?

Eugenie turned to her fisherman assistant. "Beryl," she said. "Do you know how to catch a shark?"

He gave her a funny look. Eugenie soon found out that Beryl could catch almost anything in the sea that moved. He got to work right away making a shark fishing line.

Dr. Heller and his wife came to the lab to help catch the shark.

Soon Beryl had the line ready. Steel chains made it strong. Big steel hooks on the line were baited with fish. Beryl set the line two miles*out from the shore.

First thing the next morning, Eugenie, Beryl, and Dr. and Mrs. Heller went out in the lab's boat to check the line.

The first hook was empty.

The second hook was empty.

So was the third.

"Look at this!" Beryl shouted. A steel chain was twisted. The thick metal hook was bent out of shape.

Beryl kept on pulling in the line and putting new bait on the empty hooks. Suddenly the line became hard

* about 3 kilometers

to pull. Dr. Heller grabbed the line to
help.

Then Eugenie saw it — a large gray
shark streaking through the water!

The shark was hooked but it was

still alive. They saw its staring eyes.
As its jaws moved they saw its sharp
triangular teeth.

Eugenie could hardly believe their
luck.

"What did you expect on a shark line?" Beryl beamed. "Goldfish?"

Before the day was over, they had caught another. Together the two big sharks weighed over 700 pounds.* It took six men to drag them up to shore. Now Dr. Heller had the shark livers he needed.

By the end of that first week, they had caught 12 more, mostly dusky and sandbar sharks.

Eugenie wanted to study sharks in captivity. The lab needed a place to keep sharks alive.

So next to the lab's dock, a big pen was built for holding sharks and other large fish.

Eugenie looked down into the waters of the shark pen where the big fish were swimming.

There was so much to learn about these fascinating fish, she thought. She could hardly wait to get started.

* about 320 kilograms

Children Everywhere

The lab continued to grow.

From the beginning, scientists came to the lab to work on their research projects.

There was a library just for books and magazines about sea life. There were 30 tanks for fish and other sea creatures. New shark pens were built.

Every day people brought in buckets filled with some swimming or creeping creatures of the sea. They brought in snakes and turtles. One man came in with an alligator almost

as big as Eugenie. Beryl made a pond
for it under the shade of a palm tree.

During the 12 exciting years she
worked at the lab, Eugenie had more
children. Now Hera and her little sis-
ter, Aya, had two brothers, Tak and
Niki.

Eugenie's children were never
afraid of the water. Before they were
a week old, Eugenie had taught them
to love the water. All of them could
swim long before they could walk.

Mama and Nobusan came to Florida
and opened a Japanese restaurant near
Eugenie and her family. When the
children were little, Eugenie's mother
often looked after them.

As they grew older, Eugenie's children spent more time at the lab. There were always lots of children around. Visiting scientists often brought their children with them. Neighborhood children liked to help at the lab. The children helped haul up sharks to be weighed. They helped pull in netfuls of fish to the beach.

Somedays it seemed that there were children everywhere — children peering into microscopes, children fishing from the docks, children looking at the books in the library.

Teachers brought their classes to visit. Eugenie talked to the school children about fish. Beryl showed them the alligator, the snakes, the turtles, and the big shark pen.

One day Beryl took a class out to the shark pen to show them Rosy, his favorite shark. The big nurse shark was at the bottom of the pen, out of sight. Beryl splashed his hand in the water to call her. He turned his head away for a moment to say something to the children. At that instant, Rosy swam up from below, lifted her head out of the water, and touched Beryl's hand, ever so gently. One of the children thought it looked as if Rosy were kissing Beryl's hand. But ever since that day, one of Beryl's fingers has been a little bit shorter.

That was the only time anyone was ever hurt by a shark at the lab.

As more and more scientists came to study, the lab got more and more equipment.

For Eugenie the scuba-diving equipment was the most exciting. No longer did she have to hold her breath to stay underwater or wear a heavy helmet attached by an air hose to a boat.

Now with a scuba tank of air on her back, she could stay in the underwater world for almost an hour to study the habits of the fish on a reef. And she could go deeper — deep down to 100 feet* or more, where the biggest fish — the sharks — swim.

"I was doing what I always wanted to do most," she wrote later, "studying sharks and other fish, with every-

* about 30 meters

thing in one place: collecting grounds, the lab, and my home and family."

But there were problems, too.

One Sunday afternoon, Eugenie was working at the lab. She looked out of the window and gasped. A little boy about four years old was sitting on the wooden feeding platform of the shark pen! And he was dangling his feet in the water! Eugenie dashed out of the lab and pulled the child to safety.

His parents were wandering around outside. They had paid no attention to the signs marked DANGER — SHARKS.

"We didn't see any sharks in the pen," they told Eugenie, "so we thought it was empty."

"There's a big shark swimming there right now," Eugenie said. "You're lucky it ate all it wanted yesterday or your boy's dangling foot might have been part of its dinner to-day!"

Another morning when she came to work, Eugenie found a tiger shark dead in the shark pen. A round hoop had been jammed over its head. Someone had climbed over the fence and killed it.

New signs marked KEEP OUT were posted all over and a fence was put up.

"Everyone has a lot to say about sharks attacking people," Eugenie thought sadly. "But what about people who attack sharks?"

Who Said Sharks Are Stupid?

Eugenie kept on learning new things from the sharks they caught on the shark lines. They caught hammerheads, black-fin sharks, small dogfish sharks, lemon sharks, nurse sharks, bull sharks, and tiger sharks. Once in a while they caught a great white shark.

Eugenie's success in keeping sharks in captivity became known far and wide. Scientists from all over the world were coming to the lab to study sharks.

They cut open the stomachs of sharks to find out what sharks ate. They learned that sharks ate over 40 kinds of fish, including eels, stingrays, and other sharks. They found that sharks also ate octopus, crab, and shrimp. Sometimes they ate a sea turtle or a seabird or, once in a great while, a porpoise.

Eugenie found the most interesting part of her work was studying live sharks. She got to know the sharks so well that she could tell one shark from another by its behavior.

Eugenie wanted to learn more about their feeding habits. "How much food does it take to keep a nine-foot* lemon shark alive?" Eugenie wondered. She learned that it took only two pounds** of food a day to keep it healthy and active.

One day a Dr. Lester Aronson came

* almost 3 meters
** about 1 kilogram

to the lab. His work was the study of animal behavior.

"Has anyone ever made a study of the learning behavior of sharks? Eugenie asked him.

He told her no. He said that everyone thought sharks were rather stupid.

"But you certainly have a good set-up here for testing to see if they could learn a simple task," he told her.

That was all she needed to hear. Before the day was over, they had worked out a plan.

First they designed the equipment to train the sharks. They made a wooden square and painted it white.

Eugenie placed the wooden square, called the target, into the shark pen. A shark had to learn that if it pressed its nose against the target, it would get food as a reward.

In a couple of months Eugenie's sharks learned to press the target every time they wanted food.

Then she made the test harder. First a shark had to press the target

as usual. Then it had to turn and swim to the other end of the shark pen to get its reward.

Eugenie's plan worked! She proved that sharks could indeed learn a simple task.

One day toward the end of December, Eugenie learned something else about sharks. She set up her experiment as usual. But the sharks didn't press the target. Had they forgotten everything she had taught them? It turned out that sharks lost interest in food when the water got colder.

In February, when the water in the shark pen warmed up again, the sharks began once more to press the target for food, as if they had never lost a day of practice.

Now Eugenie knew that sharks were indeed smart enough to learn. And that they had a good memory as well!

A Visit to the Palace

One summer, Dr. Aronson's 16-year-old son, Freddie, came to work at the lab. He was especially interested in setting up experiments that would help people learn how sharks use their eyes. Could sharks tell light from dark? Could they tell the difference between horizontal stripes ≡ and vertical stripes ||| ?

Freddie worked with Eugenie Clark for three summers. With the help of two other high-school students, Freddie designed new equipment with several targets to test the shark.

He trained a little two-foot* nurse shark to swim to the one target that was lit and press it when it wanted food. The shark learned in five days — a new record.

In the fall of 1965, just as Freddie was about to return to school in New York, Eugenie received an invitation to come to Japan. Her book, *Lady With a Spear*, had been published there. It was one of the most popular books in the country. She was asked to appear on TV shows. Japanese scientists wanted her to visit their labs. And best of all, the Crown Prince wanted to meet her! Like his father, the Emperor, Crown Prince Akihito was interested in fish and marine biology.

"What do you do when you are invited to the palace of the Crown Prince?" Eugenie wanted to know.

* about 60 centimeters

"You take him a present," her friends said.

"But what do you give a Prince?" She turned to Freddie. "How about your trained shark?" she said as a joke. "I'm sure the Prince doesn't have one!"

Freddie thought it was a wonderful idea. So did everyone else.

"I'll make you a special box for the shark," Freddie said. "Everything will be easy to carry."

He stayed up all that night. By morning the box was finished. It was just the right size for a two-foot shark. It was as big as a large hat box. The box was lined with plastic and filled with enough water to cover the little shark.

Eugenie was worried. "Suppose the shark dies on the way? Suppose I walk into the palace and say to the Prince, 'Here's a trained shark for you!' And suppose the shark doesn't perform?"

By now Eugenie was so worried that she was almost sorry she had accepted the royal invitation.

But everyone else was excited about a shark traveling to Japan as a present for a prince.

The airline sent men to help with the shark. The shark had a seat on the plane next to Eugenie at no extra cost. When the plane stopped in

Hawaii, the director of the aquarium there even arranged for the shark to have a swim in one of his tanks!

As the plane approached the airport in Tokyo, Eugenie took a last peek at the shark. The shark seemed fine, but Eugenie's heart was fluttering like a butterfly.

She closed the cover, and with trembling hands she carried the shark off the plane.

A huge welcoming party was waiting for her. There were scientists and professors, newspaper reporters and TV cameras. A giant truck carrying a huge saltwater aquarium stood by. The little shark that had traveled halfway around the world in a box looked even smaller swimming around in an aquarium built for a 12-foot* shark!

A special aquarium had been pre-

* about 3½ meters

pared for Eugenie's shark at the palace.

Eugenie was still nervous as she was led to the palace. With many bows and with great ceremony, she was presented to the Crown Prince.

The Crown Prince made Eugenie feel comfortable right away. He asked her many questions about her work and Eugenie forgot to be scared.

The Prince was eager to see the shark perform. It had been moved to a low tank set on top of a table in the middle of the room. Now the Prince could get a really good look at the shark.

Curtains were drawn to darken the room so that everyone could see the lighted target. One of the palace servants stood by, with a platter of reward food for the shark. Eugenie

thought it looked like food fit for the Prince himself. Slices of lobster were beautifully arranged in the shape of a flower.

Everyone was ready. Eugenie's heart was beating fast. Would the shark be able to perform?

The shark swam around the tank. Then it headed straight for the right target — to the one that was lit up.

Eugenie gave a sigh of relief. The Prince and his court clapped their hands. With jeweled chopsticks, the servant placed a slice of the lobster flower before the shark.

After that, the Prince showed Eugenie the palace aquarium. Then it was tea time. Together they sipped tea and ate cookies and talked about fish.

Eugenie was surprised to learn that the Prince had never learned to dive, had never even looked at fish through a glass face mask.

Two years after her visit to Japan, she got a telegram. The Crown Prince was passing through the United States on his way home from South America. He would like to stop in Florida and see her.

Eugenie thought the Crown Prince would be tired after his long trip. But they talked and talked about fish for hours. The other men in the room were half-asleep.

At midnight, the Prince asked her, "Dr. Clark, would you do me a favor?

Could you teach me to dive?"

"When do you want to learn?" she asked him.

"How about five o'clock this morning?" he said.

And so a few hours later, just as the sun was coming up, Eugenie taught the Crown Prince many things, like how to spit in his mask to keep the glass from fogging and how to empty the mask if it filled up with sea water.

There was only a short time left for a swim in deeper waters.

On the beach, the Prince's royal guards in rolled-up pants watched with worried faces as the American "shark lady" and Japan's Crown Prince disappeared beneath the waves.

Into the Caves of the Sleeping Sharks

Soon the happy days at the lab were over for Eugenie. Her mother had died. Eugenie's marriage had come to an end and she decided to move north with her children. Her stepfather, Nobusan, followed soon after.

Eugenie knew she was leaving the lab in good hands. Dr. Perry Gilbert, who made important studies on sharks, became the new director.

The next years were busy for Eugenie. She wrote a book about her exciting years at the lab, called *The Lady and the Sharks*.

Eugenie Clark's long-ago dream of becoming a teacher came true. She became Professor of Zoology at the University of Maryland. She shared her great knowledge and her love of fish with her students. Her students brought their friends to hear Professor Clark talk about her underwater adventures in faraway places.

"Study what fascinates you the most," she told her students.

As for herself, she never stopped studying and learning. There was always an important project to work on, something new to discover, or some underwater mystery to solve.

For instance, there was the mystery of the "sleeping" sharks.

Eugenie had her first clue from an old friend, Ramon Bravo, an underwater naturalist and photographer from Mexico. He sent word that big sharks had been discovered in an underwater cave, 67 feet* below the sea. These sharks seemed to be sleeping!

"They are not the slow-moving nurse sharks often found in caves," he told her, "but streamlined 'man-eating' requiem sharks."

Would she come and see for herself?

If it were really true, it certainly would be amazing, Eugenie thought. Everyone, including scientists, thought these sharks had to keep moving to keep water flowing over their gills. Water contains oxygen that all sharks need to stay alive.

Eugenie could take only a few days away from her teaching to go to Mexico.

When she got there she dived to the underwater cave. She saw many beautiful fish in the cave but there

* about 20 meters

were no sharks inside the cave. Then just as she was coming out, a shark slipped into the cave.

"I don't know how I can prove to you that these sharks do sleep in these caves," Ramon said. "Maybe I have to put them in pajamas and give them an alarm clock." He begged her to return as soon as she could.

The next year she was back with a research team made up of several of her students, Mexican divers, underwater photographers, and her 19-year-old daughter, Aya.

This time she saw the sharks in the caves.

"It was really unbelievable," Eugenie wrote in *National Geographic* Magazine. "There I was, face to face with one of the sea's most deadly denizens, in the most dangerous situation possible — the shark, crowded, backed into a corner — and I'd never been more thrilled. It was an unforgettable moment in my life."

There was so much Eugenie wanted to learn. The Mexican divers told her that these sharks could be touched, even lifted gently, without becoming dangerous.

Sometimes when they were poked, the sharks would swim away. Sometimes, they settled back to their sleeplike state again.

Why? Why do big, streamlined sharks stop swimming and go into this sleep-like state? From her studies, Eugenie knew that it took more energy for a streamlined shark to *stop* swimming than to keep on swimming. When a shark is at rest, it has to work harder to keep the water flowing through its gills.

Eugenie and her assistant searched for answers in the caves.

They noticed that the sharks in the

caves were very clean. Their skins were free of *parasites*, tiny animals that grow on the skins of big fish.

One day Eugenie saw a little remora fish cleaning a shark in a cave. The remora was going in and out of each gill opening, removing parasites. Then it nibbled away parasites all over the shark's head and down the shark's big body!

Could these caves be cleaning stations for sharks? It certainly looked like it.

There was so much to learn and so little time left. In a few days she had to be back at the University.

Anita George, one of Eugenie's graduate students, wanted to get some last-minute information on the sleeping sharks in the cave.

Two divers went down with her to the underwater cave. Anita took notes on her special underwater clipboard.

One of the divers flashed a bright light to take a picture with his underwater camera. Perhaps it was the light that did it. The shark woke up! It swept toward the opening of the cave, smashing its tail into Anita. It almost knocked off her face mask.

The shark was coming right toward her! She had only one thing with which to defend herself — her clip-

board. And she used it to push the big shark aside!

That night nobody got much sleep.

Time was up. There were no more days left for new adventures, or to find answers to questions.

The mystery of the sleeping sharks was still a mystery.

The Puzzle of the Sleeping Sharks

The next summer Eugenie and her assistants came back to the sleeping shark caves of Mexico.

Would they find the answers to the mystery of the sleeping sharks this time? Their tests had shown that the water in the caves *was* at times different from the water in the open sea. There was more oxygen, for one thing. And fresh water was seeping up into the caves from streams under the ocean floor.

"Perhaps there is something in the

water to make the sharks groggy," Eugenie thought.

"Perhaps our 'sleeping' sharks are drawn into the caves first to get cleaned, and second to enjoy the pleasant sensations," Dr. Clark wrote.

And did the sharks really sleep in the caves? The more Eugenie studied them, the more she thought they didn't. When Eugenie and her assistant were in the caves, the sharks' eyes followed their every move.

Eugenie wanted to find out more about the sharks' sleep-like state. "Do fish sleep the way we sleep," she wondered, "the way other animals sleep?"

"It's very difficult to make tests on fish," Eugenie said. "We're still working on ways it can be done with sharks in captivity and with sharks in the open sea."

Eugenie wrote in her *National Geo-*

graphic article: "Perhaps in deeper waters, in other parts of the world, requiem sharks also sleep."

She was right. In 1976, Eugenie was invited to Japan again. A graduate student, Anita George, came too, and this time Eugenie took along her step-father, Nobusan. He was over 70 years old and was a wonderful help. He spoke Japanese and he also learned to keep charts of the breathing rates of sharks.

Eugenie and her assistants dived in many places. In one bay Eugenie and Anita saw over 100 sharks! — more sharks than they had ever seen before at one time. Some were swimming around in the shallow end of the bay. Eugenie and Anita stood in the water taking notes while sharks swam around them.

Some of the sharks were in under-water caves, piled on top of each

other, and they seemed to be asleep!

Eugenie found two different kinds of "sleeping" sharks in Japan. One of them was a white-tip requiem shark. But what about the other white-tip reef shark, the sluggish shark that spends a good deal of time on the bottom of the reef? Perhaps there were other reasons why this shark got into a sleep-like state. More tests had to be made, more sharks studied.

Once a scientist took her to see 30 sharks in another underwater cave not far from Tokyo. Eugenie swam around, petting them, and they didn't wake up. The scientist made her promise she would never tell where the cave was.

"If people in Tokyo knew about this place," he said, "they would all race down here to hunt sharks for food."

"And people say sharks are killers," Eugenie said. "Isn't it odd that people kill and eat more sharks than sharks eat people!"

At the end of the summer, Eugenie returned to her classes at the University.

"Where will you go next to solve the mystery of the sleeping sharks?" her students asked her.

"I hear that in the Red Sea there is a cave." Eugenie's eyes sparkled. "And in that cave there are five sleeping sharks. They are the white-tip reef shark, the same kind of shark I saw in Japan. This summer I'll go back to the Red Sea.

"It's like a puzzle," Eugenie told her students. "You think you have the pieces put together and then, suddenly, one piece doesn't fit, and you're off on something else."

A Mighty Shark
and a Little Fish

Several years earlier, Eugenie had gone to Israel to do research at the Marine Laboratory on the Red Sea. She was studying a little fish they called the Moses sole.

The first time she caught the Moses sole in her net, she was surprised to see a bit of white milky fluid oozing out along its fins. She reached out and touched the fins. The milky stuff felt slippery — slimy. Her fingers felt tight and tingly. That milky fluid might be poisonous!

Eugenie made tests in the lab, and then she began experiments in the sea. She put the Moses sole in a large plastic bag that fit over a branch of coral where many little fish lived. Next she squeezed the Moses sole through the plastic bag. She squeezed until a few drops of milk came out. In minutes, every small fish that had been swimming in the bag was dead, killed by the poison of the Moses sole.

What would happen to bigger, more dangerous fish, she wondered. She began testing the Moses sole with sharks in the lab. She tied the little fish to a line in the shark tank.

First the sharks swam toward the Moses sole with their mouths open, ready to gobble the little fish. Then, with their jaws still wide open, the sharks jerked away. They thrashed and leaped about the tank, shaking their heads wildly from side to side. All the while, the Moses sole kept swimming, as if nothing unusual was happening.

Next, Eugenie put ordinary fish right next to the Moses sole on the line. The sharks kept away from those fish, too.

For the next test, Eugenie washed the skin of a Moses sole with alcohol. She dropped the fish into the shark tank. The little fish was inside the shark's stomach in no time! Washing the fish with alcohol removed its poison. So did cooking it. After it was cooked it was safe to eat.

What was this powerful poison? The little Moses sole didn't look very special. It looked like any flounder you might see in the supermarket.

Eugenie read that its milk had first been reported in 1871, over a hundred years ago. But nobody knew it was poison until Eugenie's discovery.

The Moses sole certainly kept away sharks in the lab's tanks. Now what would happen with big sharks in the sea?

Eugenie and her assistants set out shark lines in the sea, far from shore. They baited the line with different kinds of fish, some alive and some dead. All along the line, in between the other fish — but not too close — they hung the Moses sole.

They set the line during the day. Nothing happened in the daylight hours. Then the sun began to set and the sea darkened.

Eugenie and her assistants put on scuba gear and slipped into the water to watch.

The sea was calm and as smooth as glass. Suddenly the water rippled over the shark line. One dark shadow drifted up from the deep. Then another. From the dark depths of the sea, sharks were swimming up. Silently, swiftly, they swam to the little fish wriggling on the line.

The sharks ate up all the fish one by one — all but the Moses sole!

Day after day Eugenie repeated the test. She noticed that the sharks came to the line most often at dusk and again the next morning, before the sun rose. Each time, they avoided the Moses sole!

One evening, Eugenie's student, Avi Barnes, was swimming along the place where the reef drops down like a wall.

Avi signaled to Eugenie to press the button on the underwater camera. The camera lights flashed in the dark sea. Inches away from Avi was a large requiem shark — right near his head!

Eugenie could see the shark's eyes gleaming. She felt goose bumps on her arms. But the shark was not interested in Avi. There were more tempting things for it to eat — like the fish on the line.

And once again, Eugenie saw the shark gobble up all the fish on the line — all but the little Moses sole.

Naftali Primor, one of Eugenie's students in Israel, studied the effects of the milk of the Moses sole. The poison from this little fish has proven more effective than any other chemical shark repellent. A thimbleful of the milky poison could keep hungry sharks away for many hours — 18 hours in one of the tests. It doesn't wash away in the water like other chemicals.

A company that makes suntan lotions heard about the Moses sole and the vice president phoned Eugenie

Clark. The company had made a suntan lotion that doesn't come off in the water. Now they wanted to make a product that prevented sunburn *and* shark attack — all in one tube.

Eugenie is glad that a useful shark repellent might come from the little fish. But she doesn't think that the Moses sole should be used *only* as a shark repellent. She says that sharks aren't as dangerous to swimmers and divers as most people think.

There is another chemical in the milky fluid of the Moses sole that can stop the action of poisonous snake bites, scorpion bites, and bee stings.

Eugenie Clark thinks that if research companies are willing to spend the time and money, they might find a way to manufacture this chemical and save the lives of many people who are bitten by poisonous creatures, even on land.

A Shark Lady's Dream

So many dreams have come true for Eugenie Clark. When she was a little girl, she dreamed of walking on the bottom of the sea with fish, swimming with sharks, and becoming a teacher. Later she dreamed of working at her own Marine Lab. All those dreams really did come true.

She has traveled widely, exploring the underwater world beneath many seas. She is still learning and making important scientific discoveries.

Eugenie Clark has won medals and

honors for her work. She has written two books and over a hundred articles.

Everywhere she goes, she makes new friends. She sees old friends, too, like Norma, her childhood friend. She still visits the Crown Prince of Japan, and Jacques Cousteau. Eugenie Clark was one of the few women who was invited on an expedition on board the *Calypso*, with Cousteau and his crew.

In Japan, Eugenie Clark is treated like a famous star. They have shown TV specials about her adventures. Strangers on the street stop her and ask for her autograph.

When Eugenie is home in Maryland, she lives with Nobusan, her stepfather. He loves to cook special meals for Eugenie's friends and her children when they come to visit. The children are grown up, but they go on diving trips with Eugenie whenever they can.

Eugenie and her family love the Red Sea best. There is a special place along the Red Sea called Ras Muhammed. Eugenie thinks it's the most beautiful spot in the world. She calls it an underwater fairyland.

Eugenie Clark has worked and dived with thousands of sharks. People often ask if she has ever been attacked.

"Only once," she says.

Once the teeth of a 12-foot* tiger shark sank into her arm and made it bleed. But the accident didn't happen in the water! She was driving to a school to talk to children about sharks. Beside her, on the front seat, was the dried and mounted jaw of a tiger shark. The traffic light turned from green to red. She stopped short and slammed on the brakes. She

* about 3½ meters

stretched out her arm to keep the mounted jaw from falling off the seat and the jaw fell against her arm! It was the only time a shark's teeth ever bit Eugenie.

What does she want to do when she gets old? people ask her.

"I want to keep on diving." Eugenie says. "I hope I will still be diving when I'm 90!"

A letter from Eugenie Clark

Dear girls and boys,

I love my work and I never stop learning about the sea and its creatures.
Scientists agree that there is always
so much to learn and so many new discoveries to be made.

Some of you might want to be marine
biologists, oceanographers or ichthyolo-
gists, and share my delight in the wonders
of the sea. Some of you might not want
to be scientists at all.

Whatever you grow up to be, I hope you
get great satisfaction in your work and
that you get involved in what interests
you the most.

Sincerely yours,

Eugenie Clark

Other books by Ann McGovern:

Christopher Columbus
If You Lived in Colonial Times
If You Lived with the Sioux Indians
If You Grew Up with Abraham Lincoln
If You Sailed on the Mayflower in 1620
Wanted Dead or Alive: The True Story of Harriet Tubman

SCHOLASTIC BIOGRAPHY